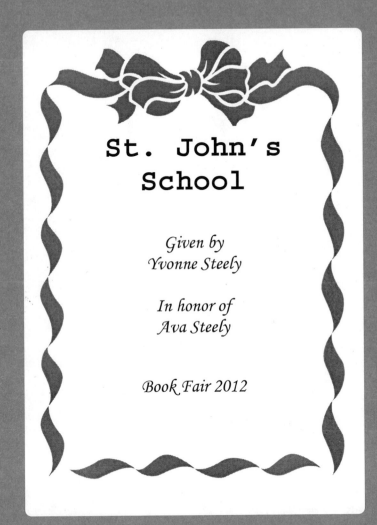

St. John's School

Given by
Yvonne Steely

In honor of
Ava Steely

Book Fair 2012

TEXAS
Aesop's
Fables

TEXAS
Aesop's
Fables

By David Davis
Illustrated by Sue Marshall Ward

PELICAN PUBLISHING COMPANY
GRETNA 2008

For my daughter, Amoreena, and my grandchildren, Ashley, Kayla, and Tyler. Also to editors Nina Kooij and Lindsey Reynolds, Caitlin Smith, and John Scheyd.—D. D.

To my sons, Joel and Mike. You gotta love 'em.—S. M. W.

The word "Pelican" and the depiction of a pelican are trademarks of Pelican Publishing Company, Inc., and are registered in the U.S. Patent and Trademark Office.

Library of Congress Cataloging-in-Publication Data

Davis, David (David R.), 1948-
  Texas Aesop's fables / by David Davis ; illustrated by Sue Marshall Ward.
      p. cm.
  Summary: Resets more than thirty familiar fables in a Texas setting, with such titles as "The Coyote and the Mustang Grapes" and "The Cowpoke Who Fooled His Friends," and such morals as "An hombre is judged by the bunch he rides with."
  ISBN 978-1-58980-569-9 (hardcover : alk. paper) 1. Aesop's fables—Adaptations. [1. Fables. 2. Folklore.]
I. Ward, Sue Marshall, 1941- ill. II. Aesop. III. Title.
  PZ8.2.D283Tex 2008
  398.2—dc22
  [E]

                              2008006333

Printed in Singapore
Published by Pelican Publishing Company, Inc.
1000 Burmaster Street, Gretna, Louisiana 70053

The Skinflint

One time over in Cherokee County there was an old skinflint who was tighter than a pair of cheap boots. He didn't trust banks, so he took his greenbacks and bought a big lump of gold. He buried the gold next to a gum tree on his north forty. Every morning he rode out and dug it up. He'd moon over it a spell and think about how rich he was. Then, he'd cover it up until the next day.

His hired hand noticed the old miser's strange routine and trailed him to the spot. That boy's eyes bugged out when he saw that gold. Now, this hired hand was as crooked as a dog's hind leg. He hotfooted it out to the spot with a shovel and in two shakes of a lamb's tail he had the gold and was hightailing it to Nuevo Laredo.

When the skinflint saw the empty hole, he was fit to be tied and pitched a hissy fit. A cowpoke happened by. He said, "Partner, what's got you so riled up?"

"Some sorry varmint stole the chunk of gold I kept buried in this hole. What'll I do now?"

The cowpoke said, "That's easy. Bury a big rock in the hole and pretend the gold is still there. The rock will do you just about as much good. You didn't have the gold anyway because you weren't doing anything with it."

Moral: A feller who won't use his gifts is no better off than a feller who hasn't got any.

The Coyote and the Crane

A coyote got a bone caught in his throat. He figured a crane could get it out with his long bill and spotted one fishing along the edge of Salado Creek. "I'll pay you a heap of money if you'll snatch this bone out of my throat," said the coyote.

The crane quickly agreed. He stuck his head in the coyote's mouth and jerked the bone out. "Alright, coyote," said the crane. "I did my part—now pay me."

The coyote grinned and clicked his teeth. "Listen, *amigo*," he said. "You've done been paid. You're the luckiest crane in Texas. How many critters do you know who poked their head into a coyote's mouth and lived to tell about it?"

Moral: If you work for somebody as crooked as a bucket of snakes, don't expect anything good to come of it—and feel lucky if you get away without getting hurt.

The Chief and His Sons

A wise Cherokee chief had three sons who were always fighting with each other. They kept the whole village in an uproar. One day the chief called the boys to him. He gave each an arrow. "Break the arrow in half," he said. Each boy broke his arrow easily. The chief nodded. Then, he took three more arrows and tied them in a bundle. "Now, break these arrows," he said to each in turn. Try as they might, the three boys couldn't break the bundle. The chief said, "Listen well, my sons. If you are divided amongst yourselves, your enemies will be able to snap you like an arrow." Then he held up the bundle of arrows. "But, if you stand together, no enemy will be able to harm you."

Moral: A tribe divided against itself cannot stand.

The Braggart

One morning at the New Summerfield general store, a stranger joined the farmers warming themselves around the potbellied stove. They swapped tales about one thing and another. Now this stranger was a real windjammer. No matter what the other fellers had done, he'd done better. If they raised fat hogs, his had been fatter. If they got forty bushels of corn an acre, he'd gotten eighty. If somebody had traded for a fine horse, he'd traded for a better one. After a while the stranger asked the clerk, "How about a cup of coffee on credit?" The clerk looked him up and down and said, "Buddy, that big ego—and a dollar—will get you one."

Moral: If you're good at something, folks will know it without you telling them. If you're not, bragging won't make it so.

The Coyote and the Goat

A coyote being chased by hounds jumped down a well to hide. After the dogs passed, he realized that he couldn't get back out. Directly, a goat wandered by. The goat spied the coyote down in the well and asked, "Is that water any count?"

"Any count?" the coyote said. "This is the best dang drinking water this side of Sequin!" He sipped and smacked his lips. "Jump down and take a swig. There's a'plenty!" (Of course the wily coyote didn't mention he was trapped.)

The goat, thinking only about a drink, hopped down the well. He guzzled water till he liked to have busted a gut. After the goat finished, the coyote said, "Goat, we're in a tight spot. We're stuck in this well." He grinned. "But don't worry, partner, I'm fixin' to get us out of here. You put your front feet up on the wall yonder. I'll climb out and pull you up."

The goat did as the coyote said, and the coyote climbed up his back and out of the well. The coyote took off running. The goat yelled, "You sidewinder, come back and keep your side of the bargain!"

The coyote yelled back at the goat, "It's your own fault you're in a fix. Before you jumped in, you should have looked to see if there was a way out."

Moral: Don't be fooled by slick talk
and look before you leap.

The Tortoise and the Jackrabbit

A jackrabbit from Archer City bragged to all the other critters about how fast he could run. He said, "I'm faster than greased lighting. I can beat any *hombre* here, hands down." He noticed a tortoise plodding along and hoorahed him about his stubby legs. "Grandmaw was slow, but she was old!" the rabbit said. "What's your excuse, *amigo*?"

All the other varmints laughed. The tortoise walked up to the rabbit and said, "You're mighty full of yourself, long ears. Listen, if you've got the sand, race me to Tumbleweed Flats tomorrow."

"Sure thing, pilgrim," said the jackrabbit. "Get a good look at the front of me now, 'cause my back is all you'll see when the race starts. I'll get to Tumbleweed Flats before you even get fifty yards."

Every critter from here to Mineral Wells lined up to see the race. It took the tortoise thirty minutes just to get to the starting line. The jackrabbit taunted him. "You're slow as cold molasses!" he said. The tortoise paid no attention.

The judge fired the starting gun.

"I'll see you at the finish line!" yelled the jackrabbit. "Eat my dust!" He rocketed out of sight. The tortoise coughed at the dust kicked in his face but plowed straight ahead, never looking to the right or to the left.

Down the way, the jackrabbit saw some friends sitting around a campfire.

"Come sit a spell," they said. "We've got a fresh pot of coffee."

"Don't mind if I do," said the rabbit. "I'm in a race—but it ain't much." Meanwhile, the tortoise walked straight ahead.

After chewing the fat a while, the jackrabbit ran a little farther. A pretty rabbit gal waved him over. "Hey, handsome," she said. "We're throwing a fiesta at our hacienda. There's guitar

music, barbecue, and I don't know what all. Stop by and dance a fandango or two."

"I'm in a race," the jackrabbit said.

The girl batted her eyes. "You mean you're afraid a little old slowpoke tortoise is going to catch you?"

The rabbit stood up straight. "Me? I can beat him running backwards. Let's dance!"

Meanwhile, the tortoise walked straight ahead.

The jackrabbit danced a fandango, ate four plates of barbecue, and slurped down three plates of chili beans. After he washed it down with a glass of sweet iced tea, he patted himself on the stomach. "I'm full as a tick!" he said. "I think I'll rest my eyes a few minutes." He plopped down and snored like a freight train.

Meanwhile, the tortoise walked straight ahead.

When the rabbit woke up, the sun hung low in the sky. "I slept longer than I planned, but it doesn't matter. I must still be way ahead of that shelled galoot."

The jackrabbit jogged along whistling a tune and thinking about how much fun it would be to brag about his victory. When he got to the hill overlooking Tumbleweed Flats, he couldn't believe his eyes. "Why, that tortoise is almost to

the finish line!" The rabbit blazed down the trail faster than he'd ever run before.

Meanwhile, the tortoise walked straight ahead.

"The rabbit's a'coming," yelled the judge at the finish line. "Look at him run!" The tortoise didn't look back. He just put one foot in front of the other. The jackrabbit sprinted past in a cloud of dust—but he was a second too late. The tortoise had crossed the finish line.

All the critters allowed as how that was the all-overest race they'd ever seen in those parts. They cheered and clapped the tortoise on the back. The jackrabbit's ears fell, and he slinked away without a word. As for the tortoise, he hoofed home and ate a big steaming bowl of menudo.

Moral: Slow and steady wins the race.

The Mules and the Hired Hand

Two mules pulled a heavy wagon full of watermelons along a country lane. The farm hand driving the wagon moaned and groaned. "It's hot as a jalapeño today. I ain't paid enough, and I won't get home from the Poteet Farmer's Market before dark. All I do is work, work, work!" After listening to this whining for miles, one of the mules had a bellyful. He looked back and said, "Boy, why don't you dry up? We're the ones pulling the wagon. All you're doing is driving."

Moral: Those who do the least bellyache the most.

The Cowboy and His Dog

One morning a Hondo cowhand woke up mad as a scalded cat because he had overslept. He saddled up and rushed out of the corral. He saw his border collie stretching by the gate. "Don't be so lazy," the cowboy yelled. "We've got work to do. Get a move on!" The collie said, *"Amigo,* I'm not the one who's late. I've been waiting on you here since before sunup."

*Moral: A lazy galoot blames
everybody else for his troubles.*

The Hound and the Cottontail

A hound jumped a cottontail rabbit. After a long chase, the rabbit made it into the brush and got away. A cowpoke who watched the chase laughed, "Woo-wee, hound, that rabbit sure outran you." The hound answered, "Why does that surprise you? I was just a'running to catch dinner. That cottontail was going to be dinner."

Moral: Necessity makes heroes.

The Cat and the Border Collie

A tomcat curled up in a hayloft spotted a border collie passing through the barnyard. Making the most of the situation, the cat taunted him. "You fleabag! You're the homeliest critter I ever saw. If you fell in the creek, it would run ugly for a week." The border collie calmly looked up at the tomcat and growled, "Come on down here and say that."

*Moral: Situations sometimes favor
the weak over the strong.*

The Rancher's Wife and the Bluebonnet

A rancher's wife was cleaning out her attic and came across a book of poems her husband bought her years ago when she was a young girl. Inside she found a pressed bluebonnet he'd given her along with the book. She held the flower up and smelled the faint fragrance that still remained. She smiled as she remembered that day.

Moral: The memory of a good deed never dies.

The Boys and the Frogs

Some boys playing by Mud Creek decided it would be fun to shoot at frogs with their sling-shots. They winged three or four and stopped for a moment to gather more stones. One of the frogs hopped on a lily pad and yelled, "Boys, please stop chunking rocks. It may be fun for you, but it's killing us."

*Moral: Think about how your
actions affect others.*

The Boy and the Buzzards

Down Goliad way, there was a boy who could run like a deer, but he wasn't satisfied. He envied the buzzards he saw circling in the sky. "Running is nothing," he said. "I want to fly like those boys."

He pestered the buzzards everyday. He'd yell, "How about giving me a ride up yonder?" Finally, to shut him up, they agreed. The buzzards swooped down and grabbed him. Now, this boy was pretty stout and they strained as they lifted him into the air. When they got up about fifty feet, they were plumb tuckered out. "I got a hitch in my get-a-long," one buzzard yelled. "Let's ditch this yokel!" said the other. With that, they dropped the boy into a stinking pig wallow. The boy walked home smelling like a bucket of rotten eggs.

Moral: Be careful what you wish for—you might get it.

The Boy and the Rock Candy

A boy with a nickel ran into the Muleshoe general store. "How much is your rock candy?" the boy asked. The clerk said, "A nickel a handful." The boy paid his nickel, and the clerk held out the jar. The boy reached in and grabbed so much candy in his fist, he couldn't get his hand out. Instead of settling for a little less, the boy pulled his hand as hard as he could. He jerked the jar out of the clerk's hands and it shattered on the floor. The angry clerk shooed him out the door. He said, "Boy, if you weren't so greedy, you'd have a nickel's worth of candy. Now, you've lost the candy and the nickel."

Moral: A greedy young'un has eyes bigger than his stomach.

The Cowpokes and the Mesquite

Two cowboys were out riding fence in the summer near Floresville. When noon rolled around, it was hot as an oven. They sprawled out in the shade of a mesquite tree to escape the heat. One cowboy pointed up at the limbs. "This mesquite ain't worth a plug nickel. Mesquites don't bear fruit, they're thorny, and they ain't pretty like a live oak." The second cowpoke agreed. "I guess this mesquite is about the nearest thing next to nothing there is." Just then the mesquite tree interrupted. "You ungrateful no-counts! Here I am shading you from the sun, and you call me worthless."

Moral: Be thankful for your blessings.

The Milk Maid

One fine spring morning a girl walked to Sulphur Springs to sell a bucket of cream. As she strolled along she thought about what she'd do with the money. "I'll sell this cream and buy some eggs," she said to herself. "When the eggs hatch, I'll sell the chicks for enough to buy that fancy dress in the store uptown."

She began to skip. "I'll look so pretty all the boys will ask me to the dance in Winnsboro, and the other girls will just die of envy—especially Mary Lou! I'll just twirl around and act like she isn't there." With that, she twirled, lost her balance, and tripped. The cream splashed all over her, and she was last seen sitting on her bloomers in the mud.

Moral: Don't count your chickens before they hatch.

The Blue-Tailed Norther and the Sun

A blue-tailed norther and the sun argued about who was more powerful. They saw a vaquero riding along the trail to Laredo. The norther said, "I tell you what, sun. Let's see which of us can make that vaquero shed his serape." The norther blew a strong, frosty blast, hoping the strength of the wind would tear the wrap from the vaquero's shoulders. The vaquero wrapped his serape even tighter around himself. The norther blew harder, but the vaquero just hunkered down in the saddle.

"My turn," said the sun. He beamed down a warm glow. In no time the vaquero was mopping his brow. After a few more minutes, the vaquero slipped the serape over his head and put it in his saddlebag.

Moral: Gentle persuasion is better than force.

The Boy and the Yellow Jacket Nest

A boy went to help his grandpaw cook meat for a barbecue he was throwing on the Fourth of July in Abilene. They walked out to the firepit, and the old man pointed to a mesquite. "Son," he said, "don't go near that tree yonder. There's a big yellow jacket nest in it. I'll get rid of it before everybody gets here. Don't mess with it."

The old man went into the house to get some fixings. The headstrong boy picked up a rock and chunked it into the middle of the nest. Those riled-up yellow jackets stung him all the way to the house. The other kids ate barbecue, drank lemonade, and played horseshoes. The boy laid up in bed covered with poultices with his eyes swollen shut.

Moral: Stubbornness is its own reward.

The Coyote and the Mustang Grapes

One spring day a coyote trotted along Cibolo Creek looking for some vittles. "I'm so hungry, I'd eat boiled okra!" he said. The coyote spied a bunch of ripe mustang grapes hanging on a vine and licked his chops. He jumped as high as he could trying to grab them until he was plumb tuckered out, but the grapes were out of reach.

The coyote started walking back toward the creek when a mockingbird sitting on the vine asked, "What's the matter, coyote? A smart critter like you can't figure a way to get those grapes?"

The coyote said, "I could get them if I really wanted to. It's just that mustang grapes are too sour for my taste."

Moral: Folks bad-mouth what they can't have.

The Cowpoke and the Rustlers

A cowboy was riding along the Canadian River and met some cowpunchers herding longhorns. Since it was dangerous country he decided to ride along with them until they got through the territory. All of a sudden a sheriff and his posse rode down on them. "What's the trouble, sheriff?" the cowboy asked. "You boys are driving stolen cattle," the sheriff replied. "I'm running all of you in." The cowboy pleaded with the sheriff, "I'm no rustler! I just met these galoots this morning." The sheriff said, "Sorry, partner. All I know is you're riding with them."

Moral: An hombre *is judged by the bunch he rides with.*

The Vaquero and His Boots

A vaquero rode up above San Antonio looking for stray cattle. At midday, he sat down to rest along the Guadalupe River and decided to cool his feet in the water. While he was soaking his feet, he knocked his boots into the river. "I need those boots to work cattle," he said. "What will become of my family now?" He buried his face in his hands.

Suddenly the water bubbled. Up rose a beautiful lady dressed in a flowing gown. "Who are you?" the vaquero asked. "I'm your prairie godmother," she said. "Why do you look so sad?" "I lost my boots in the river," he explained. "I'm a poor man and can't buy another pair."

The lady smiled and disappeared. When she appeared again she held a pair of solid gold boots. "Are these your boots?" she asked.

"They are truly fine boots, but they are not mine," he said.

The lady disappeared again. This time she reappeared holding a pair of solid silver boots. "Surely, these boots are yours," she said.

"No, they are not my boots, either," the vaquero said. Finally, she held up his old leather boots. "Those are my mine," he said. "*Gracias.* Thank you for finding them."

The lady beamed.
"Because you told the truth, take the silver and the gold boots as well. *Viya con dios.*"

When the overjoyed vaquero rode back to town and told the tale, a tinhorn named Red decided to try his luck. He rode the ten miles to the spot and threw his boots in the river. When the lady appeared, Red claimed both the gold and silver boots were his.

"You're crooked as a can of worms, *hombre,*" the lady said. She nodded to his horse, and the horse took off running toward town. The lady pointed at Red. "You won't get the silver or gold boots—or yours either. You can walk back to town barefooted."

Moral: Honesty is the best policy.

The Chicken, the Pig, and the Trail Cook

A hen and a pig decided they'd leave the barnyard and seek their fortune on the trail. Things went well until a winter storm blew up outside Amarillo. They decided to make for a campfire they saw in the distance. When they got there, they saw an old cook brewing coffee. "Sir, can we share your fire tonight?" asked the hen. The cook eyed them and said, "Let's make a trade. You supply the bacon and eggs for breakfast and you can bed down next to the chuck wagon."

The hen was about to shake on the bargain when the pig took off running. She finally caught up to the pig five miles down the road. The hen clucked, "Who put a bee in your bonnet? All he wanted was breakfast." The pig said, "Eggs are just a donation for you. Supplying the bacon is a total commitment for me."

Moral: Walk a mile in the other fellow's moccasins before you criticize.

The Bird Dog and the Stray

A hungry stray dog smelled food and trailed the scent to a pen at a hunting camp near Texarkana. Inside, a sleek springer spaniel was wolfing down a big bowl of grub. The spaniel looked at the stray and said, "Boy, you look mighty poor. Hang around and I'll ask my master if he'll take you in. There's room for two in here—and there's good vittles every day." The stray replied, "I'll take my chances out here, partner. I don't like the looks of that locked gate."

Moral: A man who trades his freedom for security makes a bad bargain.

The Scout and the Tenderfoot

An Indian scout hired on to guide a tenderfoot through the Big Bend country. It was cold and the tenderfoot blew into his hands. "What are you doing?" asked the scout. "I'm warming my hands," the tenderfoot explained. That evening they made camp. The scout watched the traveler blow on his cup of coffee. "Why are you doing that?" he asked. "I'm cooling my coffee," said the tenderfoot. The scout got up, mounted his pony, and started down the trail. "Where are you going?" asked the surprised tenderfoot. "I'm leaving," said the scout. "I don't trust a man who blows hot and cold in the same breath."

Moral: Let your yes mean yes and your no mean no.

The City Mouse and the Country Mouse

The Country Mouse invited the City Mouse for supper. "Come on in, boy!" said the Country Mouse. "Sit yourself down, partner, and have some frijoles." The City Mouse turned up his nose at the plate of pintos. "Listen, cousin," he said. "You're wasting your life out here in the sticks. Come with me, and I'll show you some real living!"

The Country Mouse took him up on the offer.

They traveled to town where the City Mouse lived in a fine brick home. As they scampered inside, the City Mouse warned, "Watch out for traps." The Country Mouse felt his heart in his throat as they picked their way past the deadly contraptions.

The City Mouse led the way into a huge banquet hall. "Here we are," he said. They scampered up on a long table, and the Country Mouse saw a

wonderland of rich food. There were cheeses, fruits, vegetables, breads, meats, and even a big dish of caviar. "Help yourself," laughed the City Mouse. The Country Mouse was just starting to take a bite of Longhorn cheese when they heard a noise. "The cats!" screamed the City Mouse. "Run for your life!" The mice hightailed it to a small hole in the wall just ahead of two cats. The City Mouse whispered, "Don't worry, cousin, we'll finish dining when the cats leave." The Country Mouse said, "Boy, I've enjoyed about as much of this as I can stand! I may live in a barn and eat simple food, but it's safe, and I can rock in the porch swing of an evening without worrying. I'm going back to Cherokee County."

Moral: Better a plate of beans and peace than fancy living and danger.

The Goose That Laid the Golden Eggs

Once there was a couple who farmed a little spread down near Seadrift. Every fall when the wild geese flew south for the winter, one goose stopped overnight by their small pond. Before she flew off the next morning she always left a golden egg on their doorstep. After several years, the farmer's wife grew discontent. "I want to be rich like the folks in Houston," she said. "Why don't we trap that goose and we'll get gold eggs every day instead of just once a year." The next fall, the farmer trapped the goose and put her in a coop. The goose was so unhappy living in a cage that she never laid another egg.

Moral: The greedy often wind up with nothing.

The Saddle Tramps and the Peaches

Two saddle tramps drifted out west of Fort Worth to Parker County. Toward sundown one said, "I'm so hungry, my ribs are rattling." Just then, he noticed his friend was gone. Directly, his sidekick galloped back with a hatful of peaches. "Where'd you get them?" he asked. "We'll sure make a good meal of those." "We, nothing," yelled the sidekick. "Get your own. I picked 'em, and I'm eating 'em."

Just then a farmer appeared yelling, "Stop, thief!" The tramp with the peaches moaned, "Partner, we're in a heap of trouble now!" His partner grinned and said, "What do you mean "we," *amigo*?"

Moral: Those who stick with you in bad times should have a share in the good times.

The Cowpoke Who Fooled His Friends

During a cattle drive, a cowboy got angry because he had to watch the outfit's *ramuda* while the rest of the cowboys got some shuteye. He decided to get even. Every night, after the crew bedded down, he yelled, "Horse thieves!" The other hands would come running and find nobody there but the trickster. "I sure put one over on you boys!" he'd laugh. After a week or two of this, the outfit quit paying him any attention. Down the trail one night, some rustlers did turn up. The cowboy yelled for help, but the crew ignored him. The rustlers got away with every horse the outfit had.

Moral: Nobody believes a liar even when he tells the truth.

A Tale of Two Stockmen

Two stockyard men in Fort Worth bought cattle to ship back east on the railroad. The first offered the trail bosses a fair price for their herd. The second skinned the cowboys on every deal and left the herdsmen with barely enough profit to break even. The first year the greedy stockman made the most money, but the next season, no outfits would trade with him. The trail bosses sought out the stockman who gave them a square deal—and everyone made a living. Every cattleman in Texas respected him. The greedy fourflusher's name became a byword for greed; he eventually went broke because no cowboy would sell him cattle.

Moral: Always leave something on the table for the other man.

The Man with Two Sons

An Austin feller had two sons. One became a farmer, and the other raised cattle. The man wanted to help both prosper. He decided to visit their spreads. He rode by the sodbuster's place first. "What can I do to help you?" he asked. The farmer said, "Papa, help me mend my fences so cattle don't trample my crops." Later that afternoon he stopped by to see the cattleman. He asked him how he could help out. The cowpoke said, "Papa, help me cut some fences, because my cattle need open range to graze." The old feller said to himself, "What do I do now? If I help one son, I'll hurt the other." He returned to town without helping either.

Moral: You can't please everyone.

The Farmer, the Mule, and the Horse

A farmer down Azle way owned a palomino saddle horse and a plow mule. The farmer loved the fancy horse and enjoyed the way folks watched him ride down Main Street on Saturdays. He brushed the horse everyday and built him a fine stall. The poor mule had to make do with a cold, leaky shed. The farmer cut down on the mule's feed so he could buy the horse a fancy saddle and a silver bridle. Finally, the underfed mule got too weak to pull the plow, and the farmer's crops failed. The horse, mule, and farmer nearly starved to death the next winter.

Moral: Many times those with the least respect are the most important.

The Medicine Show Horses and the Dog

Two medicine show scalawags sold worthless tonic for a dollar a bottle over in Ozona. Since several folks got sick after drinking it, the sheriff, the mayor, and an angry mob decided to make sure they left the area. That night, they put the medicine show barkers in their wagon and followed them all the way to the city limits.

As they were passing through town, the medicine wagon horses proudly high-stepped along. One of the horses noticed a dog by the way and said, "Dog, look how important we are. The whole town has turned out to see us, and we have the place of honor leading this parade!" The dog replied, "You boys aren't leading a parade—these folks are running you out of town."

Moral: Fame and respect are
two different things.

The Lawyer and the Prospector

A Dallas lawyer decided to travel to West Texas on business. Somewhere past Ranger, he got lost. He met an old prospector and his mule resting by a small creek. "Say, old-timer," he asked, "is this the trail to Amarillo?" The prospector said, "I don't rightly know." "Well," the lawyer asked, "can you tell me if this other trail will take me to Wichita Falls?" The prospector scratched his head. "I can't say for sure." Finally, the lawyer asked, "Can you at least tell me how far I've come from Fort Worth?" The prospector shook his head. "Sonny, I couldn't tell you." The lawyer yelled, "You worthless old geezer! You're not any smarter than that old mule of yours!" The prospector grinned and said, "Maybe not, but I ain't lost."

Moral: A feller needs horse sense
to go with his book learning.